R**____ ___**
SECRETS IN
Doodles

C000253991

REVEAL THE
SECRETS IN
Doodles

Patricia Marne

W. Foulsham & Co. Ltd.
London • New York • Toronto • Cape Town • Sydney

Patricia Marne is Founder Member and Chairwoman of The Graphology Society and she has written several other books which you may enjoy.

Know Yourself 1978

Graphology 'Teach Yourself Books'. Hodder & Stoughton, 1980 (Fourth Impression 1986)

Crime and Sex in Handwriting. Constable. 1981

The Secret's in Their Signature. Foulsham. 1986

W. Foulsham & Company Limited
Yeovil Road, Slough, Berkshire, SL1 4JH

ISBN 0–572–01427–9

Copyright © 1987 Patricia Marne

All rights reserved.
The Copyright Act (1956) prohibits (subject to certain very limited exceptions) the making of copies of any copyright work or of a substantial part of such a work, including the making of copies by photocopying or similar process. Written permission to make a copy or copies must therefore normally be obtained from the publisher in advance. It is advisable also to consult the publisher if in any doubt as to the legality of any copying which is to be undertaken.

Printed in Great Britain by
St Edmundsbury Press Ltd, Bury St Edmunds, Suffolk

CONTENTS

AN INTRODUCTION TO DOODLES

A doodle is a design or 'picture' scribbled whilst one thinks of something else. Yet, like any other form of writing, it reveals many traits of personality. Most doodles are drawn subconsciously, and therefore what we doodle is a good indication of our hopes, fears, desires and dreams.

There are many types of doodle: abstract, realistic, dots, squares, geometrical patterns, animals, human faces. Each picture tells a story and supplies a clue to the emotional thought patterns of the scribbler, bringing to the surface many surprising facets of his or her character.

Defining the word 'doodle' has proved difficult for the dictionaries. They have been called Nonsense Pictures, Diagrams of the Subconscious, or just plain scribbles. But whatever we call them, they certainly tell us a lot about the persons who drew them.

Some psychologists regard doodles as projections of repressed emotions and thoughts, and they are often used in assessing personality as an aid to psychoanalysis.

Even the would-be amateur psychologist can try and interpret the secret meaning behind these scribbles that relatives, friends, management or staff may doodle in an idle moment.

The executive at the conference table, the typist at her shorthand pad, the secretary and the P.A. at the telephone — all can betray their personalities and their subconscious wishes when they have a pen in hand and start doodling.

Basically, doodles are symbols something like dreams, occasionally concealing emotional feelings and secret desires.

Like dreams they are not easy to interpret, but can be helpful by providing clues to the doodler's emotional influences and experiences that lie beneath the surface.

There are many common symbols whose meaning is so obvious they need no deciphering. Among them are the romantic hearts and flowers, squares and grilles of those feeling trapped, and also geometrical formations indicating an ability to extricate themselves from difficult situations and deal with complexities with ease.

Symbolism is also seen in ships, planes, cars — all revealing an urge to escape in travel.

Symbolism is not hard to define once one knows what to look for. Complicated doodles often require psychological analysis as well as graphological.

Carl Jung made great use of doodles as an insight into the human mind, realising that man has always drawn or scribbled pictures to express his anxieties, and happiness, often on the walls of caves. Even today many prehistoric pictures and paintings survive, symbolising fighting, hunting, the human figures in various roles, monuments to the need of man for self expression.

Egyptian hieroglyphics were perhaps the beginning of doodles as symbols representing the inner thoughts of man.

Almost everyone doodles — there are a few exceptions — but a doodler in a preoccupied mood, coming across a pen or pencil on a writing surface, will use this to reveal his subconscious mind.

Many large companies and organisations spend thousands of pounds a year removing the damage done to toilets and staff rooms by lipstick, pen or pencil. Library books also have a fascination for doodlers, who scribble in the margins and underline words, or add question marks.

Agencies who are security conscious destroy memos and scribbling pads at the end of each day's work as they know the value of such nonsense pictures in revealing secrets that could be useful to an enemy.

In moments of tension or frustration doodles can, in fact, release these feelings and even rescue hostile thoughts by projecting the anger into graphic images.

Whatever your feelings towards doodles as projections of emotions and thoughts, they make an amusing and entertaining psychological test, bringing the thought pattern of the doodle to the surface and releasing unconscious dreams, perhaps held for years, or some repressed experience from the past.

A non-aggressive person is likely to scribble round curved doodles. If you draw circles and light pressured pictures, you are exhibiting neither anger nor frustration. They generally show a loving and affectionate nature. The doodler is sensitive, receptive and able to co-operate with others. The heart often rules the head.

An aggressive person will doodle sharp lines, angles, spiky strokes, arrows or thin formations with pointed ends. The pressure is likely to be heavy and dark, and the doodles may even be underlined. The head controls the heart.

People who repeat the same doodle over and over again may have a slight compulsion neurosis. A variety of doodles reveals a versatile and active mind.

Occasionally it may be necessary for a graphologist to have some idea of the doodler from association in order to interpret his or her doodle.

Most of the great psycho-analysts used doodles as an insight into the human mind, and many psychologists still do. Freud and Adler as well as Jung were fully aware of the significance of graphic expression in doodles or drawings, and they gave them a place in psychology along with other psychological tests.

THE VARIOUS TYPES OF DOODLE

Aggressive

Angular or spiky doodles with sharp pointed strokes are a sign of aggression and sometimes anger and frustration. They are often doodled by males rather than females and indicate a certain amount of hostility. When the pressure is heavy and dark this can represent suppressed anger and tension.

Romantic

These are shown in forms that have rounded strokes, little hearts, flowers and rings, representing the eternal love without end. They symbolise a basically non-aggressive doodler who is often in love with love. These are more likely to be doodled by female doodlers, particularly young girls.

Social

Faces are a sign of sociability of lack of it, they are an example of how the doodler deals with relationships and other people. Faces pointing to the left indicate reserve and introspection, while faces right are likely to show a more outward going personality and need for companionship and communication with others. A full face shows a friendly, extroverted personality who needs to live and work within the framework of people. Watch out for those grumpy or distorted faces; they can mean that the doodler isn't too happy with his present life.

Dollar signs and pound symbols indicate that the doodler may be too preoccupied with money matters and materialistic things.

You will be trying so hard to keep up with the Joneses you might just neglect those close to you who are far more important. It could be that you are dealing with money matters in your job or career and are inclined to be a little obsessed with it.

If doodles are chaotic and lack any shape or form but are erratic scribbles, the mind is in some sort of conflict and you don't know which way to go. There is a big decision to make and you could even have come to a turning point in life. These filled in doodles with their oddly formed shape show a mild fear or anxiety is bothering the doodler. Any filled in or heavy pressure is a sign of anxiety and difficulty in bringing those fears out into the open.

Repeated profiles represent personal thoughts and feelings of a social nature. They are an expression of the doodler's associations whether good or bad in his social life. When the profiles are happy, smiling and friendly they show a contented nature, and when they are gloomy, grumpy or unpleasant they may reveal the opposite.

Little flowers, animals and leaves are often a sign of fertility when seen in female doodles. They represent sometimes unfulfilled longings and wishes and are, of course, usually very non-aggressive, showing the more sensitive and sentimental side of the doodler.

Pictures of trains, ships and moving objects reveal a desire for travel and adventure; they are frequently expressing pent up feelings for escape and flight from everyday situations and tasks.

In doodles lie the clues to both positive and negative sides of the personality and doodlers will begin to understand themselves a little more by studying them.

If you want to try and analyse your own doodles read the contents of this book first and use it as a starting point to help you in your quest for more knowledge of yourself and your friends.

THE MEANING OF
<u>COLOUR IN DOODLING</u>

Colour is important in doodling analysis, but it should be remembered that the choice of pen is often due to the pen available at the time of doodling. The significance is heightened when a certain colour is constantly chosen. This can reveal quite a lot about the personality of the doodler.

Red: This is a cardinal sign of sexuality and energy. It represents anger and aggression and a disposition that is highly stimulated.

Pink: Shows a feminine attitude and a more receptive and passive personality with a need for harmony, especially in the emotional area.

Blue: Signifies a spiritual and more reflective nature and a desire for a friction-free existence.

Yellow: A symbol of money matters and materialism. Often a seeking for security and good health.

Brown: This is a down to earth sign indicating a

common sense nature and a strong need for emotional and environmental security.

Green: Symbolic of resentment and a wish to be different, it also shows a degree of jealousy.

Black: This depressing colour can indicate a certain amount of anxiety or tension. When chosen as first colour, it can mean that the doodler is suffering from mild feelings of depression.

Mauve: Not a usual choice of colour, but when used frequently, it shows sensitivity, a desire for achieving wish fulfilments and emotional inconsistency.

A COLLECTION OF DOODLES AND THEIR INTERPRETATION

This doodler has a slightly sarcastic manner and sometimes is very definite in her views and opinions. She has a positive personality and is not easily swayed by other people. She likes to be orderly and she has a flair for management. In addition to her many intellectual and spiritual aspirations, she is perceptive and has a very active imagination.

This young man has an off-beat sense of humour and a sense of fun. He is basically kind and friendly; there is a slight laziness at times indicated, and he likes to relax.

He is a sensualist and enjoys the material things of life and doesn't mind showing it. Careerwise, he can be consistent; he has a constructive mind, is a little aggressive in this sphere and he can plan.

He sometimes gives serious thought to a wide range of interests and he can offer excellent criticism.

There's quite a lot of ambition showing in this exaggerated word with its crossed lines and filled in edges. It shows a humorous and versatile mind, and the cloud-like formation round the word reveals a soft approach to important issues. Confident and with a conscientious attitude towards his work, this doodler enjoys variety and change. Routine and a rigid environment are not for him. A typical male doodle expressing a somewhat erratic and yet disciplined creativity.

Fertility symbols can be seen in these small S-like formations. They are foetus-shaped and show the doodler's preoccupation with children and her need for them. The light pressure reveals a delicate and sensitive nature, the roundness of her strokes a need for love and harmony. These doodles are a classic example of wish fulfilment in a woman who is wrapped up in motherhood and the desire to procreate and produce.

Arguments and quarrels are meat and drink to this doodler who enjoys a good verbal fight. The arrows indicate aggression and stubbornness, while the starlike centre reveals a highly ambitious individual with the tenacity of purpose to get what she wants. Secretive, diplomatic and concealing her true thoughts and feelings, she is clever and analytical with a cool, composed, slightly calculating character.

Money symbols in handwriting, either dollar signs or pound signs, often reveal a love of money or money power, the possession of riches being a desired goal of the doodler.

Being money conscious, this doodler also shows he carries his obsession even to the point of incorporating it into a name.

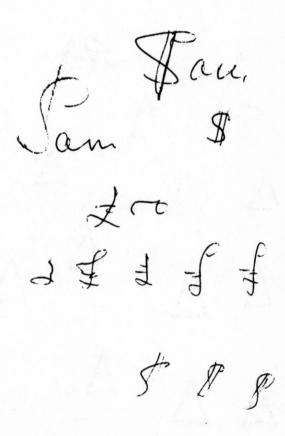

Triangles formed in series, pyramid-style, show an aptitude for constructive work and thinking. This doodler is able to make decisions quickly and is a man who enjoys solving logical problems. An individual with a down to earth approach, he shows good organising ability but isn't likely to be too tolerant of people who stand in his way as he likes to dominate his area of influence. Those pointed tops are a sign of aggression.

These filled-in and shaded doodles show a degree of tension causing the doodler to live an active inner life and shun social activity through apprehension. Emotional experiences in childhood have influenced her behaviour which is inclined to be introverted and without much self-confidence. The four little circles trapped in her circle reveal a poor little ego trying to get out but the feeling of inhibition is preventing her from expressing her personality.

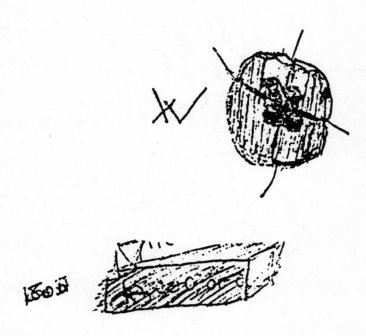

This doodler is showing a dislike of conformity. He reveals muddle-headedness and poor organising skill. Symbolic of a chaotic thinker who cannot reason logically or with any sort of method, the doodle shows he is erratic, with no defined line to follow. The lack of precision and any kind of structure demonstrates his hasty and confused thinking. Always in a hurry, this doodler doesn't give himself time to think before plunging into action. The pressure denotes physical energy for sustained effort which is misplaced.

A sense of fun and an off-beat humour is seen in these odd little faces with their weird shaped ears and hair. The doodler likes to be different and the sun shining above his faces is a sign of optimism and hope. Because of his rounded strokes he is kind, sentimental and has a socially minded disposition but the pipe in the mouth warns people not to come too close unless he says so. The glasses, too, are an indication of mild defensiveness according to mood.

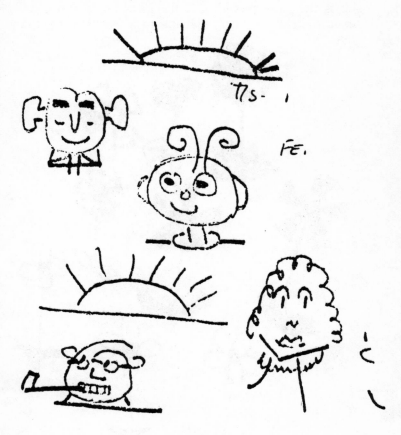

It's rare to find heavy pressure on flowers but these dark, brooding roots and leaves show depression. The doodler finds it hard to lighten her thoughts and is feeling extremely heavy hearted. The filling in reveals a certain sadness, yet the rounded flowers and strokes indicate that she hasn't completely lost her sense of beauty and her spirits are capable of rising above her troubles once she finds the way to let them loose.

The fact that the doodle is at the top of the page shows that she goes off into flights of fancy and lacks a sense of reality at times, living in a world of her own creation.

Filling in of letters shows neatness and order; the doodler likes a place for everything and everything in its place. She is inclined to be a bit of a perfectionist even to the point of finishing other people's tasks and demonstrates a mentality that is symbolic of a need for space and unrestricted movement. The pressure is a sign of bursts of temper under tension but this is usually kept well under control and she rarely gives way to her anger. A reasonably uncomplicated personality with a sense of responsibility.

Very hurriedly drawn.
Dread to know your
interpretation!
I mostly do the ones
b + c.

These question mark symbols indicate versatility and initiative. They show a quirky sense of humour and, although the doodler has a great sense of the absurd, he can be very rational and logical when making decisions and solving problems.

He can be a mixture of kindness and sarcasm, according to mood, and there is a certain amount of mistrust in his make-up although he is shrewd and creative but slightly compulsive when he gets an idea in his head.

The ring — a circle without an end — represents eternal love, everlasting and true. This doodler has a need to give and receive love and affection. She is kind, friendly and without guile or aggression, but may find that she is occasionally taken for granted. She seeks harmony and unison in her love life. The joined circles show that she is rather conventional — no women's lib for this doodler — and as an uncomplicated person, she doesn't demand too much from life, only love.

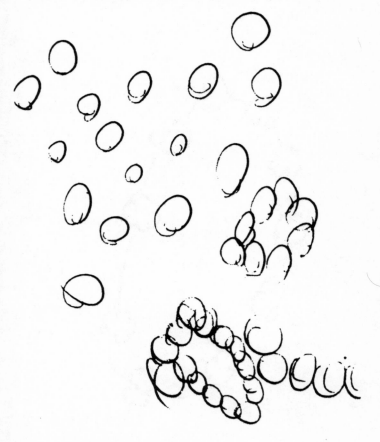

Pretty flowers in circles such as these reveal a need for escaping into day dreaming now and then. The doodler is inclined to hide from the unpleasant things of life, concentrating on nice thoughts and ideas. She is easy going, without guile and likes harmony in her domestic and family life.

Good natured and with a happy, contented disposition, she has strong family ties and enjoys showing sympathetic understanding to others.

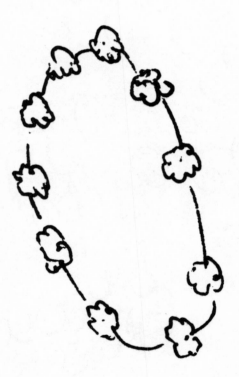

Filled-in numbers are a common doodle, particularly for those whose work or interest lies in figures or money. These filled-in figures with fine lines are a sign of a fluent thinking personality who is familiar with financial matters. The writer shows a mild fear of making mistakes, and yet is clever and quick to grasp essentials. He is, however, often held back by an innate caution that is part of his make-up.

The triangle in the form of a star with overstroked lines indicates a desire to reach the top. The doodler is energetic and a go-getter but is inclined to be a little too much concerned with unimportant issues. He may lose opportunities through this and regret his pedantic attitude to even the most mundane of things. The heavy pressure reveals vitality and an ability to sustain effort when necessary. He can also become obsessed easily and is likely to have some fixed ideas and opinions.

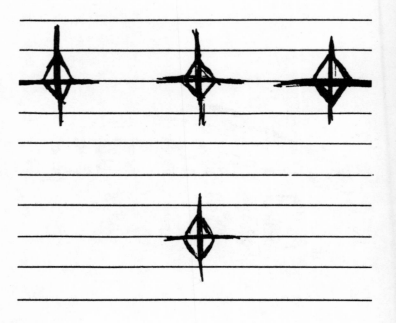

This pattern of complicated grilles and squares reveals a clever and complex mind. The doodler is feeling slightly anxious and isn't using all of his mental agility as he would wish. The angles and thin strokes are a sign of aggression and sarcasm, often a defensiveness. He is a touchy man, difficult to convince once his mind is made up. The suppressed anger he shows in his doodles is caused by environmental tensions he finds hard to cope with. His analytical approach to everything makes him a keen observer.

This left profile of a girl indicates shyness on the part of the writer who wishes to project an image of herself. The face is basically intended to be glamorous and the style of the hair shows a desire for sexual allurement. The doodler is tied to the past but wishes to mix and communicate much more than she does. The rather large lips reveal her sensuality. The fine lines of her flowing hair indicate a highly sensitive nature easily hurt and bruised by words.

Jugs, too, are a sign of sexuality in doodle analysis. Revealing a sentimental and kind nature, this simple jug with its little pattern shows an uncomplicated personality who is seeking to belong. The open top shows a generous, receptive character, warm hearted and sympathetic. She is possibly a trifle gullible in her emotional life but certainly a lady who thinks of others and enjoys helping people. A little slapdash, she doesn't stand on ceremony and is straightforward and reliable.

Doodling snakes is often a sexual symbol. They are doodled by women more than men and occasionally pent up sexual feelings are expressed in their formation. The light pressure shown here indicates that the doodler isn't capable of projecting a lot of vitality into her love life although she would like to do so. This is causing her some frustration. The letters refer to someone whose name begins with J or B who has some significance for the doodler.

This man is a methodical planner. He doesn't leave anything to chance. He has a slight feeling of frustration careerwise, and has lots of imagination and an eye for detail. There is a desire for some form of protection from the world around him and he has some minor fears and inner worries. He is a complicated man, who is often his own worst enemy by allowing himself to be trapped by circumstances through a little lack of effort. Because of the mental energy he uses he is inclined to neglect his own emotional needs.

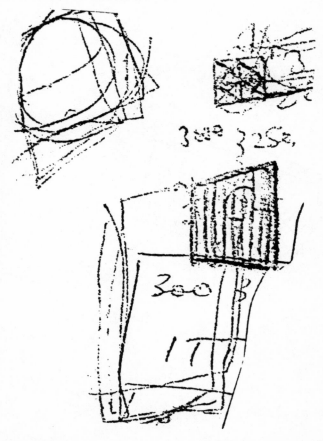

There's a little struggling ego trying to get out of this grille-like doodle. The doodler is finding it hard to escape his responsibilities and emerge as a confident person because of the rut he is in. He is searching for an identity and not having much success at the moment. The lines indicate his frustration. The tiny filled-in circles reveal his rather squashed image of self that is emerging. The figures show an aptitude for financial matters and this could be the area where his problems lie.

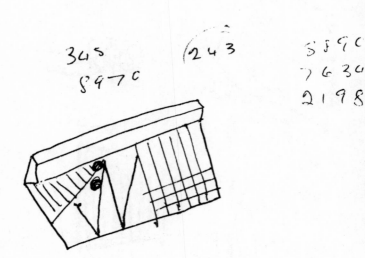

Matchstick men are frequently doodled by very ambitious executives who seek to enhance their status and prestige. They want to project a confident and successful image. They can be doodled by both males and females and are a sign of highly motivated individuals who want to make their mark on the world and in their particular sphere of influence and activity.

Somewhat abrupt and aggressive, they tend to lose touch with the needs of others so intent are they on impressing their ideas on the world. The angles and square confirm this doodler's sharpness of mind.

Movement, travel and action are displayed in this doodle. The ship is moving along the waves, showing an erratic but go ahead nature, inconsistent and restless. The doodler releases tension by getting away from it all and day dreaming. There is a lack of energy in the light pressure, stopping him from actually indulging in adventures, but he is content to let his mind wander and lives an active inner life. The smoke going two ways confirms his inability to go directly to his world of action.

Different slanting trees indicate the doodler is often torn between mind and emotion, impulse and control. They reveal indecision and a tendency to dislike making decisions. The doodler finds it hard to stick to routine and is frequently being tossed by her erratic emotions. The round, fluffy crowns show a warm, affectionate nature but a rather muddled one with a strong maternal instinct.

The fine lines show a sensitivity which could cause her to over-react to criticism although she will respond well to any form of encouragement or praise.

A sample of an expression suggesting eternal love and fidelity is seen in the circles at the bottom of the page, and the heart shape with its arrow shows a romantic who is in love with love.

Sentimental and affectionate, the doodler is a day dreamer. The initials have a special meaning to her. The arrows are rounded rather than pointed, confirming her warm-hearted and non-aggressive nature. Continuity and romance are the themes running through this doodle.

Spirals on their own or repeated indicate a desire for security — usually within the family and home. This doodle shows a tendency to regress back to childhood when life was 'safe' and the doodler felt loved and secure.

When the spiral is compulsively doodled over and over again with persistence this can reveal a certain degree of anxiety and a tendency on the part of the doodler to brood on his problems as he seeks a way out of his present insecurities.

These Christmas trees with their dark, filled in trunks reveal a slightly sarcastic nature and a sharp wit. The doodler is clever, intelligent and rapid thinking, and likes to get down to essentials quickly. The star at the top shows ambition and drive.

The writer has high aspirations, enjoys a firm foundation to live and work in and seeks a materialistic security in order to feel secure.

Not easily swayed by emotion, the doodler is mentally agile, possesses excellent head control and is capable of allowing his head to rule his heart without regret.

This doodle is drawn by an introspective man who is mildly inhibited in the emotional area. He is good at solving problems, has an analytical mind and can deal with facts. He puts up barriers against too much intrusion into his private life and affairs. Although he has ideas he wants to develop, he often takes two steps forward and one backwards through caution, instead of going ahead and aiming for his goal.

He shows a strong need to protect his ego, can be difficult to understand and needs to expand his personality more than he does. He appears to be in a rut — possibly of his own making.

A lady doodler who lives in a world of thought not things, she is a day dreamer, full of high flying ideas and is interested in animals and ecology. She is basically peace loving and non-aggressive, finds great consolation in nature and does not like any kind of violence.

The strange little objects with their clawlike openings reveal her love of animals and children.

An unusual doodle from an unusual mind, her flights of fantasy are a way of escape for her.

This doodle reveals a highly goal orientated personality who possesses push and drive especially in the career area. This is a lady with a purpose who is a thinker; she likes to push her own ideas.

She is capable of working with detail, and has an extremely good eye for detailed work. But in striving for perfection she may lose out on the emotional side of life now and then through her preoccupation with material things. There is a lot of strength in her doodle and she can put up considerable opposition to external influences which sometimes prevent her from expressing her deeper personality.

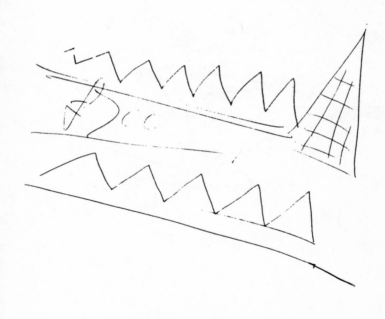

This unusual doodle — a finger pointing upwards within a maze of lines and triangles — shows a rather dominant ego and a tendency to bossiness. Ambitious, and possessing considerable self-importance, the doodler dislikes being overlooked and is conscious of his image. He is not a person to hide his light under a bushel, nor will he suffer fools gladly. The finger is accusing and somewhat rigid. He often feels that he isn't getting the recognition he or his work deserves.

What an ambitious lady Glenda is with her many pointed stars and varying squares and boxes or circles. She reveals a lot of drive and skill in organising and planning, and is fully aware of what she can do and can't. Although there is some aggression in her sharp pointed stars, there is also a romantic streak lurking in her flower and her strong-willed personality means that she is a lady to be reckoned with as she will accept a challenge and isn't afraid to make her mark.

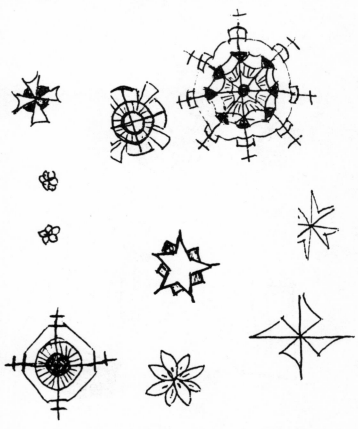

Boxes are symbols of firm foundations and security. When these doodles are drawn by women — and boxes often are — they represent a desire for order, method and safety. The doodler here shows a strongly practical mind and some constructive skill but she is also inclined to keep herself to herself and inhibit her need for companionship and a sharing relationship. There are signs of a lack of warmth in the filled-in box and some tiny fears about the future. Her rounded flower-like doodles express her emotions which are kept in check. Lying hidden is an affectionate and loving personality trying to get out of a self-imposed isolation.

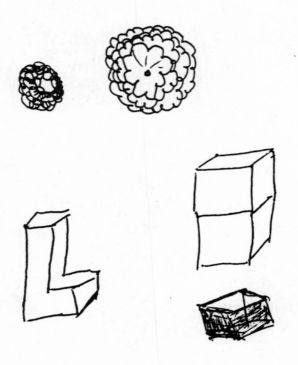

This doodler has a romantic attitude towards the senses and she sometimes feels trapped by her own emotions. She is a romantic at heart and yet had known some form of unhappiness. There is a desire for a social life shown and she likes to meet people and enjoys company.

An affectionate person, she is inclined to believe in the old-fashioned idea of love in a cottage which seems to have eluded her. The rather pensive face of the little man in her doodle with its tightly closed mouth shows how bottled up she feels at times.

There is a closing in — a wariness — about this doodle. The doodler is creative, artistic and lives in her imagination with an interest in colour and design. She is aiming for realism in her relationships and is an optimist at heart.

There is some degree of tension in her doodle, showing that she is suffering from mild insecurity in her emotional life. She is also apprehensive about losing something or someone close to her. An unusual doodle with many overtones of a complex character.

What a happy-go-lucky little doodle this is with the sun shining on a world of flowers, tiny mushrooms and the flowing wavy line of the landscape. There's no hostility here, only a sense of fun and bright cheerfulness. The tiny stars above show ambition and a go-ahead personality with high ideals and aspirations. Only a lightly doodled cloud appears in this picture to mar its contentment.

This filled in maze shows conflict as the doodler copes with problems she finds hard to unravel. The pressure is heavy in places, indicating fluctuating energy, but she seeks to relieve the gloom she is feeling and the tension she is under at the moment.

She has to find a way out of her anxieties and in the process seems to wallow a little bit in her unhappiness. The fact that she uses all of the space shows that she should be resourceful and able eventually to solve her predicament.

These ghost-like doodles are sexually inspired, showing that the doodler is preoccupied with his sexual fantasies and is expressing them graphically. The fine pressure indicates a sensitive and highly perceptive personality who possesses considerable creative ability and tends to bottle up his true thoughts and feelings. There is no hostility in the doodles, only a compulsiveness about the doodler's thoughts which seem to haunt him.

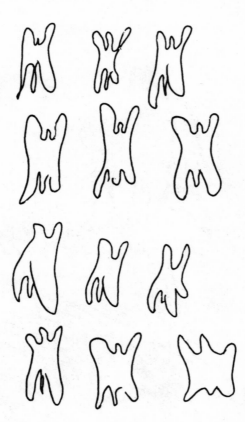

No warmth radiates from these stark branches with their lifeless leaves. They show a deficiency of warmth and feeling, any affection somewhat stunted by their sharpness. The angularity is a sign of emotional unhappiness and frustration, even mild depression in the scribbles at the bottom of the page.

A pessimistic attitude appears in the rather weary lines and the doodler doesn't have a lot of reserve energy to fall back on as his pressure is inclined to be light and frothy. The scrawls at the root of the trees show a need for a strong, solid and stable environment to function in.

Doodling cups and saucers is a feminine trait, showing a tendency to allow thoughts of sex to wander. This doodle is showing her love of security, home and husband in the rounded base of her scribbles and the spoons leaning to the right.

Her cups indicate fertility and children, her aims and ambitions all lying in the direction of family life.

Alan doodles different faces looking various ways, showing his variable moods and changing social attitudes — sometimes outward going and friendly, at other times rather introspective and inward looking.

The eyes are all drawn quite large, revealing an observant and sensitive nature with strong perceptiveness. The mouths of his faces are small, showing an ability to keep his own counsel. Alan isn't the sort of person to gossip or reveal a confidence.

The spiky hair on his faces is a sign of a good critical sense and considerable mental alertness, combined with a need for warmth and affection which seems to be missing from his life.

The pressure of his doodles is not particularly heavy, indicating sensitivity, and the size variation reveals that he frequently feels being pulled in two directions at once, especially in the emotional sphere. This may cause him to appear more diffident in his responses than he is.

Male 35 (me).

This doodler shows a basically non-aggressive nature although she can certainly stand up for herself when necessary. The rounded strokes are a sign of a need for harmony in her home and domestic life, but the slightly muddled heart of her flowers indicates that she doesn't mind a fight now and then in order to clear the air.

There is little leaning to the right in her drawings, showing her social attitude is outward going but tinged with reservation.

Not a lady to suffer fools gladly.

Intelligent and clever at solving problems, this doodler is able to express himself well and fluently; he is a constructive thinker, able to organise and plan with efficiency and vision. His emotions are kept under control and he is a cool, calculating individual with excellent powers of concentration.

A man who sums up situations with care and discrimination before making his move. In competitive spheres he's a force to be reckoned with.

Strong-willed and stubborn, this writer is a highly critical person with a degree of tension showing in her sparsely made tree with its drooping lines and crown. The branches are poorly formed and reveal little vitality. There is also a very rigid mind here and her views are inflexible. Once she has made a point, this doodler will stick by it.

The fact that her tree has a circle at the base indicates her desire for materialistic security in her life.

By keeping her tree to the left of the page she is confirming an introspective, somewhat withdrawn attitude towards other people. The circling round of her name is a sign of protection and defensiveness.

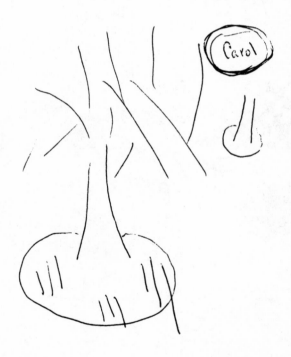

Mischievous eyes with a glint in them show a whimsical sense of humour and excellent powers of observation. There isn't much this doodler doesn't see. The rounded faces show her basically kind nature but the spiky lines indicate a well developed sarcastic streak when roused or angered.

The rather ugly face with its thin, square-like mouth reveals her ability to keep her own counsel. She is not a lady to give way to unsolicited gossip.

Highly sensitive and very definite in her likes and dislikes, she forms her impressions on first meetings.

Considerable pressure has been applied in this heavily filled in doodle, which means that the doodler is under tension and is finding it hard to maintain his position in the scheme of things. The grille-like structure is a sign of being fenced in and feeling frustrated, while the angular and box-like strokes indicate he has to fight off opposition and other people's ideas. He has difficulty in getting his own concepts to the fore. An energetic man, he needs to ease up on the stress level he is working at and relax so that his tension can begin to diminish.

Uncoordinated lines and scribbles that have no real meaning but run over the page in a mass of graphic lines show a muddled and complicated mind. This doodler is finding it difficult to make decisions, or come to any easy conclusions about her life. The light pressure shows her to be a highly perceptive and sensitive personality, one who is intelligent and basically non-aggressive as her rounded strokes indicate. By using the entire page for her scribble she is demonstrating a need for self-expression and freedom from restrictions.

Here is an easy-going, amiable doodler, good natured and with an off-beat sense of humour. He also shows a sense of fun. He is able to concentrate on detailed work and routine doesn't bother him too much. He can be logical and there is no aggression in his make-up or resentment in his doodle. He isn't easily diverted from a thing once his mind has been made up and is a great flirt with the opposite sex, his whimsical attitude attracting them.

The tiny triangles to the right of his picture tell of caution in his really intimate relationships.

Geometrically linked squares show a capacity for practical skills, the doodler having a nature demanding realism rather than phantasy and daydreams. There's a basic lack of pretentiousness in his make-up.

He likes to use his common sense and practical ability, both in his work and approach to everyday matters. Not the most romantic of individuals but one who is reliable and to be trusted.

This doodler has a desire to probe his own emotions and is inclined to be obsessed by his own reactions. He likes to watch himself taking in the inner workings of his mind. He has a good intellect, is intelligent and critical, and there is some practical ability apart from creative skill. He shows a good sense of humour and self preservation, frequently playing safe in his relationships. He often feels insecure and conceals this with a display of receptiveness towards people in order to bolster his confidence.

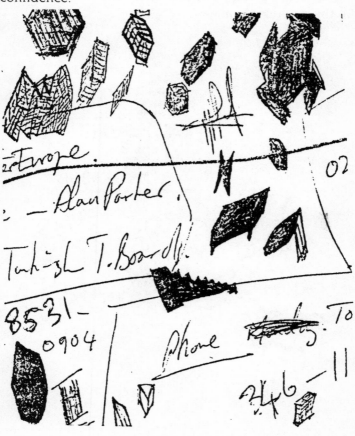

Jotting down little dots shows a cautious personality, and in these doodles there are signs of secrecy and diplomacy, the doodler preferring to look on rather than taking part in life. He keeps a discreet watch from the sidelines and is an accurate observer.

A cool, mature person who thinks much yet says little, he dislikes making a fuss over things — this is alien to his character. This type of doodle belongs to the think-ers of the world rather than the doers. The varying pressure of the dots and dashes reveals mood variation in the emotional sphere.

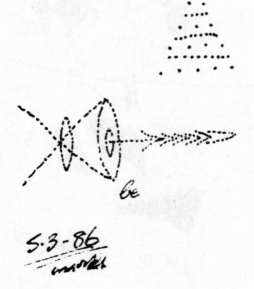

CELEBRITY DOODLES

Maureen Lipman — Actress

This doodle shows a passionate woman, intensely emotional and very much aware of what's going on around her. She likes to be with people but has a mild fear of them in case they take her over. A very private person in her personal life, she is highly perceptive and intuitive.

This doodle gives off a very sexy image, but underneath she has a strongly maternal instinct and her family comes first. She knows what she wants from life — and how to get it. She's creative and ambitious but at times hides her real feelings behind a prickly defensiveness. Not a lady to suffer fools gladly.

Ann Kirkbride

This doodler is often torn between head and heart, causing a lot of soul searching. She's a romantic, loving and needing to feel secure. She's career minded too, but isn't particularly aggressive in this area. Gentle, sensitive and appearing tougher than she is, she is a progressive thinker.

Alan Freeman — Disc Jockey

In his doodle, he shows a strong musical interest and a large ego. He plays his emotions close to his chest and is inclined to be emotionally self-centred. He has some pretty fixed ideas and opinions and doesn't like to be criticised.

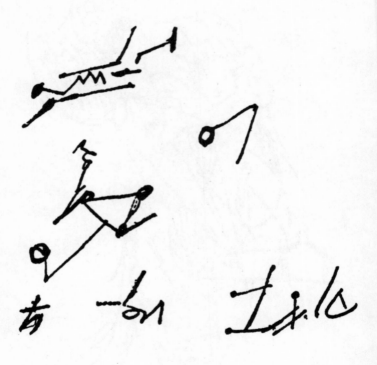

Leslie Thomas — Author of Virgin Soldiers

Leslie's doodle shows a dreamer. It represents his ideals as he is a man who needs a partner to share his dreams. He's good natured, caring and generous, but there's a hint of suspicion. He can give a wrong impression at times by hiding behind a slightly sarcastic tongue when he's under pressure.

David Essex

This doodle shows that David likes to get away from his public image and away from the limelight now and then. The large watching eye is a sign of his flirtatious but slightly suspicious nature. Although he's affectionate he tends to be a bit cautious of people who thrust themselves at him. David likes to be thought the chaser rather than the chased, and although he does enjoy admiration and attention he has the ability to laugh at himself.

He shows in his doodle that he possesses a constructive mind with the ability to make his dreams come true.

The beak-like top of his doodle shows his love of action.

The whole doodle reveals that David had some doubts about a project at the time he doodled.

Vince Hill — Singer

Vince's doodle is a fairly stark tree and lots of presents at the bottom, showing that in his early life he had to practise thrift and he is very keen on material security. The tiny angular stars show ambition and persistence, the lack of round strokes indicates his head rules his heart and he is quite a good businessman.

Robin Cousins

Robin's doodle shows that he wants to protect himself from unwanted interference in his life. His filled-in little man reveals that he is often prone to anxiety. He becomes worried when he is under tension and although the man's outstretched arms show sociability this is tinged with reserve. His need to express his personality makes Robin seem far more outward going than his true nature.

The detailed hat and scarf reveal a bit of the perfectionist in his personality.

Shakin' Stevens

His doodle shows a frantic urge to express his personality and reveals his love of movement and rhythm. The longer-flowing strokes show a love of colour and travel. Stevens has filled in his letters, showing that he's a little bit secretive and has a desire for security.

His doodle reveals his unusual mind and unique train of thought. The hot dogs underneath the letters tell that he's a bit of a dreamer and has a habit of wasting time working on small, unimportant details. By shading in his letters he shows that he is anxious about the future.

He loves space and likes to be in the middle of whatever is happening in his world, as he thrives on stimulation from new experiences and people.

Anthony Hopkins — Actor

There is a remoteness about this doodle giving it a rather isolated look. The moon is upside down, showing a wry view of life, and the small fence on the right of the page is a sign of defensiveness. A brooding picture indicating a man who thinks too much and allows his introspective nature to take over.

The large amount of space between moon and fence reveals his sense of isolation and the fact that he has placed his doodle in a frame shows his feelings of being trapped by his own thoughts and emotions.

FERTILITY DOODLES

TRAVEL AND
ADVENTURE DOODLES

WISH FULFILMENT DOODLES

SEXUAL DOODLES

ANIMALS, HEARTS AND FLOWERS ARE ALL ROMANTIC DOODLES

SOCIAL DOODLES

WEBS — MAZES AND CROSSED LINES

FEMININE DOODLES

MASCULINE DOODLES

AGGRESSIVE
DOODLES

DRAW A TREE AND REVEAL YOUR EMOTIONAL RATING

One of the most revealing things you can be asked to draw is a tree because it shows many facets of your emotional life. It can be a useful guide to gaining insight into this sphere of your personality. Your tree is divided into two parts — the crown and the trunk. Compare it with the trees shown here — you could be in for a surprise.

Bare

1. If your tree is stark, bare and without leaves on its crown, it means that you are inclined to be impatient and sarcastic with a well developed critical streak to your nature. You tend to bottle up your emotions and rarely let yourself go. Learning to relax, even laughing at yourself now and then, would work wonders for that uptight feeling. Try giving your emotions an airing and just watch that tension disappear.

Fruit

2. A tree with lots of fruit hanging from the branches shows that you are reasonably mature emotionally, have a need to love and to be loved and enjoy showing off on occasion. Basically warm-hearted and affectionate, you have a tendency to spend a lot of your time day-dreaming and often find yourself in love with love.

Round

3. A nicely rounded tree crown reveals a calm, rather placid nature — excellent at listening to other people's problems. You're kind, warm and friendly, usually reliable and thoughtful, but just a tiny bit lazy now and then. You are sometimes gullible where your emotions are concerned and, because of your faith in human nature, you have a tendency to fall for a hard luck story.

Spiky

4. Spiky and uncoordinated lines show irritability and perhaps even sexual frustration. Under tension you become touchy and have a quick temper which flares up quickly when provoked. You also have a sense of dignity and confidence in your own actions. You don't like people meddling in your affairs as this puts you on the defensive, making you more aggressive than usual.

Circles

5. Tiny circles within circles is a sign that you are under tension or under pressure. This can make you rather emotionally vulnerable because you are quick to react to outside stimulus. You have a habit of withdrawing into your own private world which makes you appear far more aloof and unresponsive than you really are. Try opening up a bit and see how easy it is to make friends.

Droopings

6. If your doodle resembles a willow tree, this is a sign of defeat and depression and a heavy heart. You are inclined to let things get you down and your pessimism makes you difficult to deal with. Moodiness is one of your greatest weaknesses and results in your family and friends having to treat you in a very cautious way in case they get their heads bitten off.

Christmas tree

7. If your doodle is like a Christmas tree, it reveals a stubborn streak in your nature. Physically very active, you enjoy the outdoor life. When you take a strong dislike to someone or something, you do not easily change your mind. You also have fixed ideas about sex and love. Yours is an unconventional nature. You are strong-willed and a great stickler for detail.

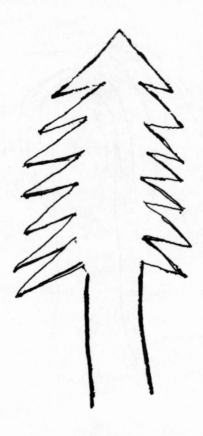

Island

8. Setting your tree on an island means that you are seeking security — especially emotional security — and you have a desire to 'belong'. Although there isn't any real aggression in your nature you can defend yourself passionately when necessary. You are a home bird — with family and friends always taking priority. Watch out that your sex life doesn't become dull and boring.

Fluffy

9. A very fluffy crown to your tree indicates that you can cope with problems that crop up in your life well. You are an imaginative person who prefers the companionship of others to your own. You have a slightly exaggerated idea of your own importance and a big ego. But you are adaptable and versatile, and with the right person — you can be very sexy indeed.

Sloping

10. Setting your tree on a hill or the side of a hill indicates a cautious nature. You can be distrustful and a bit suspicious of people. You feel rather lonely, neglected and isolated. At times you lack spontaneity which makes you appear cold and calculating. You are extremely independent and this spills over into your sexual and emotional life — often with negative results.

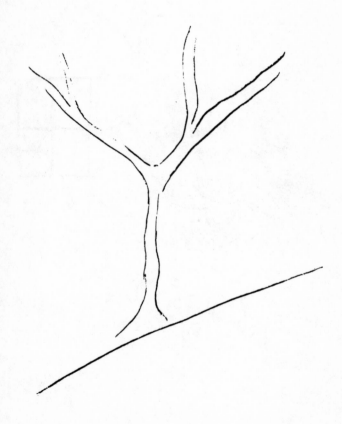

Shaded

11. A shaded tree is a sign of fear or apprehension; you could be anxious about something, or worrying about not coming up to expectations. This lack of confidence makes you feel inadequate. Bring your fears out into the open and you'll lose that feeling of living under a cloud.

Broken lines

12. Broken lines show that you are rather uncontrolled emotionally. You tend to plunge into relationships and friendships without thought for the consequences. You also have a habit of making decisions without giving too much thought to the outcome.

Long roots

13. Long roots indicate that you want security in your life and, thanks to your realistic and observant nature, you usually find it. A good balance between head and heart keeps you relatively cool in most situations. There's more than a hint of jealousy in your nature and you aren't the most trusting of personalities.

Scarred trunk

14. It seems as though you're trying to forget a bad experience your subconscious mind won't let go. You'll find that new people and plans will help erase this experience from your mind if you really want to forget.

Flared trunk

15. What an energetic person you are! There's a need for plenty of activity in your life and you enjoy being the life and soul of the party as social occasions make you sparkle. Your busy social life means that you have many friends.

Long, thin trunk

16. A long, thin trunk shows there's a little bit of snobbery in your nature. It makes you yearn for intellectual attainment, but although you are enthusiastic for new ideas, you rarely carry them out as you are easily side tracked.

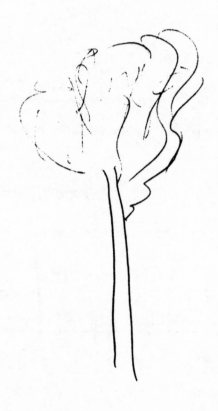

DOODLING A HOUSE

Curious to reveal that part of yourself you may not even be aware of? By drawing a house you can do just that because your version of this simple building is very symbolic: it represents your attitude to home, family and security — or lack of it.

If your house is drawn with just the bare necessities, your windows are uncurtained, there is no knocker or letter box, and your chimney doesn't have smoke coming out of it, it means you could be lacking in spontaneous affection and shows you have difficulty in establishing warm and loving relationships. You're cautious and you don't like talking about your private life.

If your house has the sun shining above it, and stands surrounded by trees, shrubs and a fence, with smoke coming out of the chimney, and curtained windows, what a happy contented individual you are. You enjoy your home and family, and haven't any real deep desires for anything else. You've drawn a healthy, well balanced picture of your easy-going, basically non-aggressive personality.

If your house is large and sprawling with a tree to the left, this indicates that you are strongly influenced by the past, particularly your family life, and are still under the influence of your family, possibly your mother. There's a need for security and protection from the big bad world and your secret wish is for a knight in shining armour to come along and offer you permanent love and security.

A house that has a roof significantly out of proportion with the rest of the building shows you are an habitual daydreamer, indulging in harmless fantasies of love and life. Your desire to find a partner to share your dreams and adventures can lead you into strange friendships, but there's a strong streak of optimism in your nature that sees you through.

A house with lots of windows and doors could mean you enjoy a gossip and like to know what goes on around you.

If you have a couple of people looking out of the windows, this means you are sociable with lots of outside interests. However, your subconscious could be telling you that what you really yearn for is a deep relationship. Love and companionship are high on your list of priorities.

Should your house be drawn near a church or with a church in the background, you could be feeling a bit down or under the weather, and need cheering up. Your deep emotions often confuse you and don't always bring you happiness.

A tendency to brood also makes you depressed at times, but take heart. Your secret wish for someone to lean on can become a reality if you wake up to your full potential.

If you draw a huge, squat house with a door that leads to a widening path in the front garden, you're likely to be the chatty, friendly, sociable type who invites friends back home. You're not particularly tactful and can't keep a secret, but your generosity and lovable personality make up for that. You like to be active and are happiest when surrounded by good company.

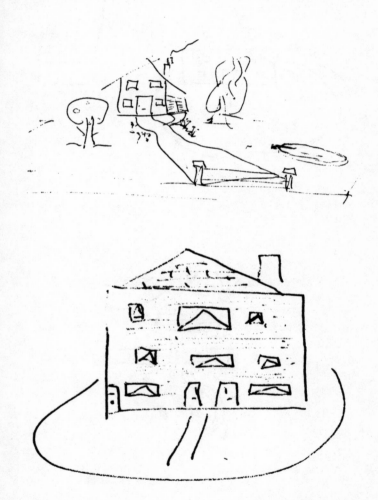

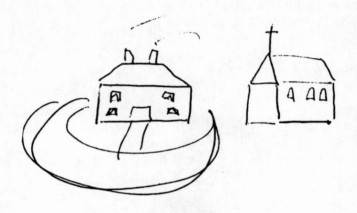

A small house, with a large garden all the way round, reveals your desire for security financially, and your love can be stifling and even claustrophobic. Although you give an impression of open-mindedness you secretly enjoy your possessions and possessiveness and have little desire to change.

A tall, thin house with slits for door and windows reveals rigid thinking and a narrow, blinkered outlook. Your fixed principles could be the root cause of your narrow mindedness therefore strangling your potentials. By opening your mind to fresh ideas and fresh ventures, you can open up a new world for yourself, as emotionally you tend to be inhibited and repressed.

If your house is shaded in or blacked out, you have secret fears lurking in your subconscious. There's a mild apprehension about the future, possibly anxiety over your partner. You often lack confidence and your negative attitude is handicapping your enjoyment of life. By bringing your fears out in the open and talking about them, you'll find they disappear.

CHILDREN'S DRAWINGS

A child's drawings can reveal a lot about his character and personality. They show the importance the child places on parents, home and family environment and can indicate if the child is happy and secure, loved and wanted, or is isolated, insecure and at odds with his surroundings.

Any tiny worries or anxieties will show up and can be dealt with at an early age. Young children mature emotionally and mentally so early these days that it is possible to analyse their drawings from the age of three.

Many psychologists and child guidance counsellors in the United States and on the Continent use children's drawings to assess potential and to trace problems and this idea is beginning to make headway in this country as more people realise the significance of these graphic scribbles and how they reveal subconscious thoughts.

Drawing skill isn't always allied to intelligence — often clever drawings go hand in hand with poor intelligence. Although drawings may not appear to have much in the way of design or even pattern, these scribbles can be extremely informative to the trained eye of the graphologist. It is also important to take into account the child's choice of colour. When a child is given the choice of coloured pen or pencil he will normally pick primary colours: red, yellow, blue or green. Should he choose black or brown this is frequently found to reveal unhappiness and mild depression.

When a child uses all of the page for his drawing he is showing an extroverted nature and a sense of being loved and wanted. His hang-ups won't be of long standing — if any — and he will show independence and sociability at an early age. But if a child's drawing is small and cramped into the very middle of the page with considerable space around it, this is a warning sign. It indicates isolation and a sense of frustration.

Drawings towards the bottom of the page are a sign of physical activity. The child's energies need to be channelled into sports, games and outdoor activities where his excess vitality can be directed constructively.

The higher the drawings are on the page the more of a daydreamer the child is likely to be.

Heavy pressure is an indication of tension and light pressure of sensitivity; most children have medium pressure. Often a child is not backward but frustrated in his aims and this will be reflected in his drawings, giving clues to where the frustration lies — home, school or outside influences.

A most revealing project is to ask a child to draw a picture of his parents. Children of one parent families usually draw the mother figure rather large in front of the picture with father either to the left or at the back, showing that the parents' roles have been reversed; it is the mother who has the most important influence on the child's life.

Children who are aggressive or begin to reveal antisocial behaviour patterns will frequently draw items of violence — guns, knives — hostile symbols which express their inner feelings.

If the child has coloured pencils or crayons, colour

choice can reveal quite a lot about his or her emerging personality.

Red shows a sense of drama and a love of attention. The child is going to have a warm, affectionate but slightly demanding nature, a vivid imagination and a need to express himself creatively or actively. Blue shows the more reflective, mentally motivated child who needs harmony and security constantly. Yellow shows optimism and green can indicate sibling rivalry.

I cannot stress enough that this guide is only accurate when the child is given a free choice of colour. Any attempt to interpret his selection must be made on this basis.

Where the child starts to draw on the page is highly significant. To the left lies shyness and reserve, a tendency to withdraw into self. He needs to be encouraged to mix with his peers as much as possible to prevent introspection as a teenager. He needs plenty of love and affection in order to feel secure.

To the right of the page can indicate the over-active child who needs constant action and movement. He likes to be on the go all the time. He should be allowed to do things with his hands so that he is kept busy and won't need to seek external influences to satisfy his restless nature.

Arrows and thin, pointed strokes, too, are often found in the anti-social child's doodles or drawings. The more rounded the strokes the more emotionally inclined and affectionate the child will be. The angular and spiky lines reveal aggression and sometimes concealed anger. The following drawings were all drawn by children under the age of ten.

Dennis 5

Dennis has no hang-ups about meeting people or communicating. His drawing covers the entire page, showing his extroverted nature and love of the limelight. The fact that he signs his name backwards, however, does show that he could be slightly lazy at times and cannot be bothered to conform.

Gary 5

Gary uses primary colours for his picture and his symbolic use of space is excellent. His drawing shows a nicely balanced attitude to home and family. His house has a path and smoke coming out of the chimney, revealing imagination and a desire to allow people to come near him. The drawing on the left is also colourful and indicates his sense of form at such an early age.

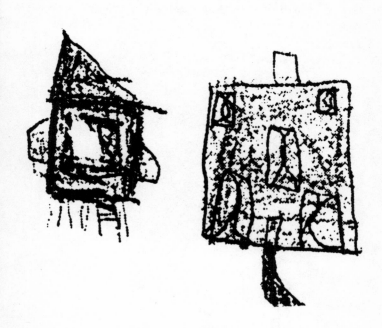

Julie 5

Julie clings to the left of the page, giving the rest of the space a miss. This indicates that she is shy, reserved, and has some difficulty in establishing contact. She leans heavily on her mother (the left side of the page is mother influence — the right side of the page more father influence). But her pressure is strong and healthy, showing good vitality. As her strokes are mainly rounded they are symbolic of an affectionate nature and she needs to be encouraged to mix and play with children within her circle so that as she gets older her social expansion will ensure that she feels more at home with people and the world.

Ann

Ann's drawing is a little sad. The fact that her house is drawn in black and she has filled in parts of her drawing very heavily tell us that she isn't too happy and feels that life is a drag. The faces without features and the house without curtains or path indicates that she is withdrawn and lacking in affection. The filling-in results from mild anxieties, and the symbolism in her drawing reveals a lack of humour and light-heartedness in her life.

John

John hasn't been able to form the outlines of his drawing well but the tendency to draw from the left to right is there and although his pressure varies a lot he shows signs of an ability to make an effort. The happy smiling face is significant and demonstrates warmth, while the emphasis on eyes in his drawing is an indication of a little wariness. There is plenty of affection and love in John's make-up and he will respond well to praise and encouragement.

Steven

Steven has a tendency to keep to the top of the page, revealing that he is a daydreamer, but he goes from left to right and there are no angular strokes, an indication of aggression. His mental agility should be directed into constructive playthings, which would prevent too much reflective dreaming and bring his thoughts down to more immediate things while allowing him to use his imagination.

David

David shows a lot of movement and energy in his drawing; speed and action are part of his personality. The emphasis on aeroplanes and trains in his picture indicates that he likes to be kept on the move. As long as he is kept busy and can channel his energies into outward-going activities he's happy. He should never be restricted in movement or freedom, even at this young age, as he is a boy with many interests which should be encouraged along the right lines. He just needs to be steered in the right direction.

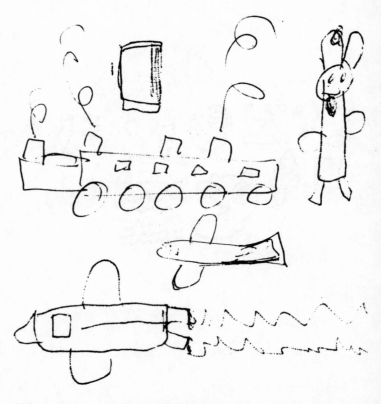

George

George is feeling down as this shows in the heavy, dark and brooding house, filled in with pressure and revealing how unhappy he is. George is coping with experiencing his first emotional problems of a sexual nature and those trees with flaring roots show that he is a bit of a realist, even at his early age. Treating him intelligently would pay off as he is very mature, and far more able to think for himself than perhaps he is given credit for.

James 5

James places his doodle bang in the middle of the page, revealing that although he wants to be in the centre of things, the space round his doodle shows he is a little apprehensive. He feels a bit lonely and needs companionship to draw him out of himself so that he can integrate well with his peers.

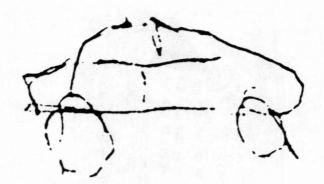

Tom

Very mild aggression shows in these arrows and daggers. However, they aren't particularly heavy or menacing and, because the pressure is light, Tom shows that he is sensitive and has quite a nice nature without too much aggression. He feels frustrated possibly at home or school and needs to talk his problems out.

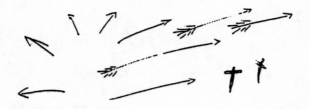

Peter 8

A little too much emphasis on the bottom of the page shows a preoccupation with the physical. Peter needs the activity that sports and games would provide to get rid of excess energy. His drawing is well designed and shows his creativity.

Michael 5

Michael's drawing shows a versatile little mind and a love of adventure. The fact that he places his drawing to the right of the page indicates that he is impatient, always seeking to charge ahead, and likes to be active. Basically non-aggressive, he is imaginative and sensitive.

INDEX